TABLE OF CONTENTS

ABSTRACT

The United States has been in a protracted war on terrorism since the events of September 11, 2001. As a result, there are ever increasing concerns over the possibility of terrorists exploiting our porous southwest border. It is well documented that the U.S. Border Patrol is undermanned, under-equipped, and under-trained to deal with the increasing numbers of illegal immigrants, escalating violent gang activity, and in the increasing incidents of questionable activity by the Mexican military. Recent televised demonstrations of millions of illegal immigrants and numerous reports of increasing border incursions have begun to alarm not only those who reside in Border States, but have also captured the attention of the nation. This paper will seek to discover through a discussion of the relevance of the Posse Comitatus Act, analysis of the growing threat on our southwestern border, the impact of placing the military on the border, and current counterargument, just how serious an issue the security of our southwestern border has become. The paper will conclude by advocating for a change in our border control policy that allows greater discretion to man the border with the U.S. Military to ensure the continued safety and sovereignty of our nation.

INTRODUCTION

"Defending our Nation against its enemies is the first and fundamental commitment of the Federal Government. Today, that task has changed dramatically."

President George W. Bush

Border security has been an area of public concern since the September 11, 2001 terrorist attacks and has trended toward even greater concern with the highly publicized rise in the numbers of illegal immigrants coming across our borders daily. As a result, there are ever increasing concerns over the possibility of terrorists exploiting our porous southwest border. Prior to the 9/11 attack, the American people and the Federal government took for granted the safety of our country's borders. In response to new threats, the Federal government has acted to pass new legislation, create new strategic policies, and stand up new organizations such as The Department of Homeland Security and NORTHCOM to ensure our nation's security. Despite these actions, little headway has been made in securing our borders. The US border, specifically, the Mexican-American border, remains our greatest vulnerability in the war on terrorism.

The current border policy as it stands today is completely inadequate to ensure our security. The U.S. Border Patrol is undermanned, under-equipped, and under-trained to deal with the increasing numbers of illegal immigrants, escalating violent gang activity, and in the increasing incidents of questionable activity by the Mexican military. If we are to prevent another event like 9/11 from occurring again, we must use the military to secure our borders. However, it can be argued that the military is already tasked with too many missions to effectively man our borders. Further, society at large may not be ready to make the necessary revisions to the Posse Comitatus Act to allow the Federal government, namely the

President, greater discretion to place the military on the border, properly empowered to deal with the full spectrum of duties associated with securing our borders.

This paper will seek to justify the need to place the military on the border by examining the relevancy of Posse Comitatus, analyzing the growing threat from the border, assessing the impact of placing the military on the border, briefly exploring a counter argument, and concluding that with the GWOT, and increasing threats to national interests from our porous southern border, that it is only logical the military assume a greater presence on the border.

POSSE COMITATUS

"Whoever, except in cases and under circumstances expressly authorized by the Constitution or Act of Congress, willfully uses any part of the Army or the Air Force as a posse comitatus or otherwise to execute the laws shall be fined under this title or imprisoned not more than two years, or both.". Posse Comitatus Act 18 U.S.C. § 1385.[1]

The Posse Comitatus Act, as written, has been a limitation on the use of military forces in civilian law enforcement operations since the Nineteenth Century. Today, where national defense may hinge on detecting smuggled biological or chemical weapons in small quantities, the continued relevance of this law is at issue. The Posse Comitatus Act is often cited as a major constraint on the use of the military services to participate in homeland security, counterterrorism, civil disturbances, and similar domestic duties. It is widely believed that this law prohibits the Army, Navy, Air Force, and Marine Corps from performing any kind of police work or assisting law enforcement agencies to enforce the law.

---

[1] Jennifer Elsea Legislative Attorney, *"The Posse Comitatus Act and Related Matters: A Sketch"*
American Law Division, Congressional Research Service Report for Congress. Received through the CRS Web

This belief, however, is not exactly correct. Title 10 U.S. Code, Chapter 18, authorizes military support for civilian law enforcement agencies for counter drug operations and in emergencies involving chemical or biological weapons of mass destruction, or any other threat to the security of our nation. Accordingly, the Secretary of Defense may provide information, allow the use of military equipment and facilities, train law enforcement officials in the operation and maintenance of military equipment, and maintain such equipment. However, support for law enforcement agencies may not impair military readiness, and military personnel shall not participate in searches, seizures, arrests, or similar activities unless such participation is otherwise authorized by law. (Military police personnel, for example, may enforce the law within their jurisdictions.)[2]

The Posse Comitatus Act is not a general and universal proscription of the use of federal military forces to enforce or execute the law. The military services may do so and have done so when ordered by the president and pursuant to the authorization of Congress. Although the current interpretation of the act is the opposite of its original intention, it does discourage the military services from being used as a national police force. However, the Posse Comitatus Act does not prevent the military services from supporting the police, nor does it preclude them from enforcing the law when so ordered by the president. It does preclude them from being the police in normal times.[3]

While the Posse Comitatus Act has effectively served the purpose originally intended, new world realities make it necessary for new rules to clearly set forth the boundaries for the use of federal military forces for homeland security. The Posse Comitatus Act is inappropriate for modern times and needs to be replaced by a completely new law. It certainly does not

---

[2] Brinkerhoff, John R. "*The Posse Comitatus Act and Homeland Securit*", February 2002. 6 p.
http://www homelandsecurity.org/journal/Articles/brinkerhoffpossecomitatus htm
[3] Ibid

provide a basis for defining a useful relationship of military forces and civil authority in a global war with terrorism.[4]

THE GROWING BORDER THREAT

The U.S. border with Mexico is some 2,000 miles long, with more than 800,000 people arriving from Mexico daily and more than 4 million commercial crossings annually[5]. The U.S.-Mexican border is the most heavily used corridor for illegal alien traffic on America's southern boundary. With its challenging topography, it is a land that yields well to smuggling. The numbers of unauthorized immigrants smuggled across the border dumbfound the imagination. As of 2001, the Border Patrol apprehended 158, 782 illegal aliens. By the Border Patrol's own admission, it only catches one in five and admits that nearly 800,000 slipped through that year.[6] Today those numbers continue to grow as evidenced by daily news reports that estimate nearly 11 million illegals currently reside in the U.S. What's even more alarming are the numbers of "Other Than Mexicans" or OTMs. In FY2004, the border patrol

apprehended 1.1 million people. The majority (94%) of these apprehensions were Mexican nationals. Because the vast majority of people apprehended each year by the border patrol are Mexican, the agency distinguishes between Mexicans and OTMs. The issue of non-Mexican nationals has received publicity recently due to Congressional testimony by DHS former acting Secretary Admiral James Loy that Al-Qaeda may be considering infiltrating the

---

[4]Ibid
[5] Lisa M. Seghetti, Coordinator, Jennifer Lake, Blas Nuñez-Neto, and Alison Siskin Domestic Social Policy Division K. Larry Storrs, Foreign Affairs, Defense and Trade Division *"Border Security and the Southwest Border: Background, Legislation, and Issues"*, September 28, 2005 CRS Report for Congress Received through the CRS Web
[6] J. Zane Walley, *"Illegal Aliens Across the Mexican Border"* Paragon Foundation, Alamogordo, NM http://www.warriorsfortruth.com/illegal-aliens-immigration html

southwest border due to a belief that "illegal entry is more advantageous than legal entry for operational security reasons." [7]

Over the past three years, OTM apprehensions have more than doubled, from 37,316 in FY2002 to 75,389 in FY2004. Ninety eight percent of this increase came from five countries, in descending order: Honduras, El Salvador, Brazil, Guatemala, Nicaragua, and the Dominican Republic. The Peoples' Republic of China showed the sixth largest increase over the three-year span. [8]

The Border Patrol has determined that at least one in ten caught is from a country like Yemen or Egypt. According to the San Diego Union-Tribune, hours after the 9-11 attacks, and anonymous caller led Mexican Immigration agents to 41 undocumented Iraqis waiting to cross into the United States. The Associated Press also reported that Mexican immigration police detained 13 citizens of Yemen on Sept 24, 2001 who reportedly were waiting to cross the border into Arizona.[9] Arguably, the most pressing concern at the southwest border is the number of undocumented aliens who still manage to cross the border every day, the majority of which are Mexican nationals. As the number of illegal aliens that are present in the United States continues to grow, attention is directed at the border patrol and the enforcement of immigration laws within the interior of the country. The Department of Homeland Security's (DHS's) Customs and Border Protection (CBP) and Immigration and Customs Enforcement (ICE) units have launched several initiatives aimed at apprehending illegal aliens and dismantling human and drug smuggling organizations. Despite these efforts, the flow of illegal migration continues. Issues such as enforcement of immigration laws and

---

[7] Ibid, p.28
[8] Ibid, p.28
[9] Ibid, J. Zane Walley, Paragon Foundation

organizational issues such as inter- and intra-agency cooperation, coordination and information sharing continue to be debated. [10]

A more serious matter than illegal immigration are the growing instances of Mexican soldiers — or criminals in Mexican army uniforms — continue making armed incursions into the US. They have boldly confronted Border Patrol and local law enforcement officers without any acknowledgement from the Bush administartion. According to a Department of Homeland Security report there have been 216 such incidents since 1996. These incursions occurred in California, Arizona and Texas. The dire situation at the border, along with the aggregate number of significant incidents in the past few years, has garnered the attention of increasing numbers of lawmakers, most notably those who represent Border States. U.S. Rep. Tom Tancredo, R-Colo., a frequent critic of the administration's border security efforts, has called for the federal government and the governments of southern border states to immediately deploy troops to the U.S.-Mexico border in light of what he termed "recent armed assistance Mexico's military has given to drug smugglers."[11] He went of further to state that "Our border has literally turned into a war zone with foreign military personnel challenging our laws and our sovereignty. The only way to deal with this dangerous situation is to tap the resources of our own military," Tancredo said.[12] Similar sentiments have been echoed by Arizona Senator Jon Kyl, chairman of the Senate Judiciary Subcommittee on Terrorism and Homeland Security, who called on Secretary of State Condoleezza Rice to initiate a formal investigation on the reported border crossings and to begin a dialogue with Mexican officials to prevent further occurrences.

---

[10] Ibid, p60
[11] Michelle Malkin. *"The War at he Border: Escalation"*, January 26, 2006 10:48 AM
http://michellemalkin.com/
[12] Ibid

"These illegal incursions are a violation of our sovereignty and pose a significant danger to U.S. law enforcement officials and citizens near the border - especially if all parties involved are armed. The potential for violence is significant."[13]

According to an article by Jerry Seper in the March 13 Washington Times, Law-enforcement officials along the Mexican border say they are outgunned and outmanned by drug smugglers armed with automatic weapons and grenades, and who use state-of-the-art communications and tracking systems. "We recently received information that cartels immediately across our border are planning on killing as many police officers as possible on the United States side" ... said Zapata County Sheriff Sigifredo Gonzalez Jr., head of the 16-member Texas Border Sheriffs Coalition. "They have the money, equipment and stamina to do it," the sheriff said. Profits made by the drug cartels also have allowed them to hire and develop what Sheriff Gonzalez described as "experts" in explosives, wiretapping, countersurveillance, lock-picking and Global Positioning System technology.[14] Most of the components of what Sheriff Gonzalez and his colleagues are facing are not new to those who follow what is known as the evolution of Fourth Generation war or asymmetric warfare. So, why are the drug and immigration smugglers on our southern border escalating the conflict? Because when they probe, they find weakness. Here we see another carry-over from the Third to the Fourth Generation, in the form of "soft spot tactics." Our border defenses, and our will to acknowledge that fact, is weak at the physical level, and at the mental and moral levels as well.[15]

The culmination effect of these events has led the nation to a point where it appears to be more than ready to embrace military involvement in homeland defense. Drug smuggling

---

[13] William S. Lind, *"On War #157: Through the Postern Gate"* http://www.sftt.org/main.cfm
[14] Ibid
[15] Ibid

and illegal immigration were perceived by some as the national defense challenges for the nineties. Since the Gulf War the military has generally received high marks from the public as an organization that is trusted and admired. That support, coupled with the increasing recognition that a suitcase of chemical or biological agent smuggled across our borders could result in a crippling loss of life, is leading to an acceptance of an increased role for the military in homeland defense.

MILITARIZING THE BORDER

Securing our borders and controlling entry to the United States has always been the responsibility of the Federal Government. The current Administration has not made explicitly clear whether it regards attacks on the United States itself as a threat which is mostly additive to the plethora of threats to U.S. national security which existed before September 11, 2001, or whether the threat to the American homeland has in fact displaced, to a major extent, the previous threats used for defining the missions, and therefore planning the size and structure, of the U.S. armed forces. This is a question of great long-term significance for the reserve (as well as the active) components. If the terrorist threat is additive, then the missions the existing reserve force structure is designed to perform, remain, and new forces must be organized to meet the new, terrorism generated missions.[16]

Currently, the military plays a very limited role along the borders, but some armed forces have been used in the past to help battle drug traffickers. National Guard units, meanwhile, have been used at times by southern and western governors to provide assistance at border crossings. However, state governors view the National Guard as a scarce resource for

---

[16] Robert L. Goldich Specialist in National Defense Foreign Affairs, Defense, and Trade Division *"Homeland Security and the Reserves: Threat, Mission, and Force Structure Issues"* September 10, 2002 p.2 Report for Congress Received through the CRS Web Order Code RL31564

Homeland Security and other aid to civil authority. Since the terrorist attacks of September 11, 2001, many have asserted that "homeland defense" and/or "homeland security" are natural, ideal, or logical missions for the reserve components of the armed forces (including the National Guard) and that reserve missions and resources should be substantially reoriented so as to emphasize homeland security. Several rationales for this assumption have been advanced, including the following: as the focus of contingency planning expands to include attacks on U.S. territory, reserve forces, because of their members' long-term community ties, will be the most knowledgeable about local conditions, problems, and special circumstances.[17] Reserve units are stationed at small armories and other facilities at thousands of locations, in major urban and suburban areas as well as rural ones, around the country. Active force units–particularly those of the Army and Marine Corps–tend to be concentrated at large bases, often in areas removed from major population centers (to provide enough space for training).[18] The statutorily-defined, and constitutionally-derived, status of the National Guard as the organized militia of each state, as well as a federal military reserve force, enables the Guard to be used within the United States without posing questions of improper military intrusion into civil affairs. However, a recent report done by the Heritage Foundation suggests that the heightened importance of homeland security demands that the entire National Guard be fundamentally restructured so that its primary mission is homeland security. The Heritage study and similar discussions elsewhere argue that the Guard's local ties and decentralized presence throughout the country makes it ideal for homeland defense missions.[19]

---

[17] Ibid, p.1
[18] Ibid, p.2
[19] Ibid, p.6

If/when the American people come to grip with the seriousness of our border security problem and conclude there is a necessity for placing the military on the border, what are some of the issues likely facing the operational commander who spearheads this effort? The most challenging issue concerns "domestic military operations". Domestic military operations require the military to operate in sensitive civilian environments under constitutional constraints, and to work with multiple civilian agencies that may have very different ways of doing things. In the past, the military has performed many civil-military activities requiring such sensitivity in the past, including support to law enforcement (counter drug operations and riot relief), disaster relief (e.g., after hurricanes), and management of immigration crises (e.g., housing Cuban émigrés at Guantanamo Bay)[20]. However, training a cadre of professional soldiers to effectively deal with the challenges of domestic security would certainly be difficult [21]

Other issues for the operational commander include resourcing, organization, and command and control. The structure to deal with these issues currently exists in United States Northern Command (NORTHCOM), which was created in the aftermath of 9-11 as a response to the emergence of these multi-dimensional threats. When NORTHCOM was created by the US Government it tasked the Combatant Commander (COCOM) with the following mission:

"The command's mission is homeland defense and civil support, specifically: Conduct operations to deter, prevent, and defeat threats and aggression aimed at the United States, its territories, and interests within

---

[20] Ibid, p.6
[21] Karen Guttieri, "Homeland Security and US Civil-Military Relations Strategic Insights", Volume II, Issue 8 (August 2003) Center For Contemp Conflict. http://www.ccc.nps navy mil/

the assigned area of responsibility; and as directed by the President or Secretary of Defense, provide defense support of civil authorities including consequence management operations." [22]

From this mission statement it is clear that border security fall under this rubric. However, NORTHCOM, unlike USSOCOM, has no forces assigned and has to depend on apportioned forces to meet mission requirements. To employ our military effectively to secure our borders, we need to assign forces to NORTHCOM. The source of this manpower lays in our overall National Guard strength. According to a fact sheet at Guard Bureau website, the structure of the National Guard maintains an endstrength of 350,000 soldiers[23]. Maintaining 15 separate brigades, these forces are currently organized into seven armored, seven infantry, and one cavalry units.[24] These forces are available to the President when federalized under Title 10 and at all other times are available to the individual state Governor's to respond in the event of a disaster.[25] This clearly could provide the manpower to enable NORTHCOM to respond if these forces were placed at the disposal of the COCOM. Of course, a policy shift such as this would most certainly cause concern among our nations governors. One way to mitigate that concern would be to increase the end-strength of the Guard to accommodate this added mission requirement. However, this is not likely to happen.

This new approach to Homeland Security and Homeland Defense would allow the Federal government to be ready to quickly and adeptly respond to a multitude of domestic missions, including securing our borders. It is incumbent on the federal government to be ready with a viable well trained force to step in at a moment's notice, not a force that has to be

---

[22] USNORTHCOM mission statement downloaded from the World Wide Web on 21 October 2005. This document goes to the establishment of the mission and the primary problem.
[23] NATIONAL GUARD BUREAU, This document directly describes the forces available and the force structure of the Guard, fact sheet, pg.1.
[24] NATIONAL GUARD BUREAU, Ibid, pg1.
[25] NATIONAL GUARD BUREAU, Ibid, pg1

federalized, then mobilized, then trained, and finally put into action, only after a state government has failed to cope. Let's assume for arguments sake, that a doctrinal change takes place wherein the federal government decides to change the size of the active duty Army to compensate for the loss of the ability to tap the National Guard for federalization and use overseas in any regional contingency. Additionally, an assumption of a direct command linkage between NORTHCOM and the Chief of the National Guard Bureau exists. This would enable NORTHCOM to plan to a standard wherein they would know that their Joint Force Land Component Commander, (JFLCC) would respond to and train to a standard of readiness and responsiveness. This, in effect, would establish a federal response force in standing. If we create a federal response structure, then the NORTHCOM commander could tap those forces from outside the area in question and push additional assets into the scenario.

We as a nation cannot allow the chaos on border regions to continue. It's clearly evident that a change in policy and approach is warranted. Unfortunately, ongoing political realities have kept the Administration from taking a more aggressive stance to secure our border. Sadly, it will likely take an event such as 9-11, whose origin is our southwest border, to move the government toward real solutions.

I suspect what has kept the Department of Defense, through NORTHCOM from executing its mission as delineated in the National Response Plan and the Unified Command Plan is that fact we continue to focus on fighting the away game, exclusively. Since 9-11, we have been very successful with maintaining an offense in the terrorists' back yard; however, if we continue to maintain the status quo, it's only a matter of time before the enemy succeeds with a CBRNE event in our homeland. I'm convinced this event is more likely to originate from our southern border than any other port of entry. Simply put, we need to adopt a new policy that provides forces to NORTHCOM so we can effectively manage our scarce manpower resources and be ready to respond to our federally mandated responsibility of securing our borders.

COUNTERARGUMENT

While many are now advocating a greater role for the US Military on the border, there are also many who view this option with skepticism and grave concern. Two of the most prevalent views concern the impact on civil-military relations and the impact on the force itself. With the establishment of a Department of Homeland Security, some policymakers advocate giving the military a larger role in protecting the home front from terrorist attack. This area seems to draw the most concern in that there is fear these trends will result in a large, semi-autonomous military so different and estranged from society that it will become unaccountable to those whom it serves.[26] "Weakening the prohibitions against the domestic use of the military will have a potentially deleterious effect on civil-military relations, military professionalism, and readiness, and most importantly, the civil liberties of the American people". [27]

While the potential impact on civil-military relations is certainly an issue for debate, the tangible impact on the force itself is a more compelling issue. Reorienting the Guard and Reserves toward homeland security missions would have a measurable impact on the active forces, and most likely reduce the readiness of U.S. forces, at least in the near term. To restructure reserve units toward homeland defense could, therefore, not only reduce their

---

[26] Mackubin Owens, *"Soldiers Aren't Cops"*, National Review on line. August 1, 2002 9:00 a.m. Makubin Owens is also a distinguished professor at the Naval War College http: //www nationalreview.com
[27] Ibid

utility for wartime missions, but reduce the ability of the armed forces–active and reserve–to carry out existing peacetime missions, most of which are integral, high-visibility components of U.S. foreign policy. [28]

The other impact on the force, and more pointedly, the operational commander, involves a fundamental lack of training for border security missions. A good example of the impact of improper training occurred in 1997 when a U.S. Marine team shot and killed a Texas teenager near the border after mistaking him for a drug scout. The soldiers assigned this mission were trained to kill, not to inform suspects of their rights. The killing led to minor changes in border enforcement policy, but not to a public examination of the militarization.[29] The U.S. military is structured to play "away games." It is good at protecting the United States by threatening the sanctuary of our adversaries abroad. There are, of course, things the military can do to enhance the security of the American homeland, but we should not be blurring further the distinction between military activities and domestic law enforcement. [30] The fundamental problem with deploying the military to the border, especially in the near term, is the same training that makes U.S. soldiers outstanding warriors makes them extremely dangerous as cops. Lawrence Korb, former assistant secretary of defense in the Reagan administration, put it succinctly: "The military is trained to vaporize, not Mirandize.[31]

---

[28] Ibid
[29] Gene Healy, " *Don't Militarize the Borders*" February 17, 2003
Gene Healy is senior editor at the Cato Institute, http://www.cato.org/
[30] Ibid
[31] Ibid

CONCLUSION

Illegal immigration and border security issues have been slowly, but surely, moving to the forefront of public concern. Massive demonstrations of illegal immigrants and mounting reports of the staggering numbers of undocumented aliens that continue to pour across our southern border have begun to alarm more than just those Americans who reside in our border states. A recent CNN report reflects this heightened emphasis on border security and supports an assertion that the Administration and the American people are moving ever closer to a solution that involves the military. The report states that due to mounting pressure from lawmakers and Governors from the border states, the Pentagon has recently begun exploring ways to lend support at the southern border. The report also describes a measure recently voted on in the House that will allow the Homeland Security Department, in limited cases, to use soldiers in that region. The vote will also allow Defense Secretary Donald Rumsfeld to now assign military personnel under certain circumstances to help the Homeland Security Department with border security. The report goes on to describe how these actions underscored the importance of the border and immigration issues, yet were deemed tentative enough to reflect worries about drawing the nation's armed forces into a politically sensitive domestic role.[32]

Beyond the posturing and rhetoric that accompany any discussion of placing the military on the border, the fact remains that border security is absolutely essential if we are to reduce the imminent threat of new acts of terrorism on American soil, maintain our sovereignty as a free and decent nation, and contain the alarming growth of international criminal syndicates that are violently overtaking our territory and assaulting our people. Clearly, federal law

---

[32] CNN.com report *"Pentagon eyes ways to use military for border security"* Friday, May 12, 2006; Posted: 10:24 a m. EDT (14:24 GMT) http://www.cnn.com/2006/US/05/12/border.defense.ap/index html

enforcement agencies responsible for securing our borders have neither the personnel nor the resources to effectively deter, detect, and apprehend the growing numbers of illegal immigrants violating our borders. The Mexican government continues to play lip service to U.S. border security issues, and their military is under continual suspicion of being complicate with local drug cartels and activities that deal in human trafficking. The U.S. Military has the personnel and the resources to effectively control the flow of illegal immigrants and to deal with increasingly well armed criminals, and renegade Mexican military militia, who pose a serious and documented threat to our border communities and Border Patrol agents. This heightened emphasis on border enforcement, and the lack of an effective civil policy, clearly demonstrates the need for a military solution to aid agencies in securing our border.

SELECTED BIBLIOGRAPHY

Owens, Mackubin Thomas. *Soldiers Aren't Cops: the case against domesticating the military.* National Review Online, August 1, 2002,
http://www.nationalreview.com/owens/owens080102.asp

Coakley, Robert W. *The Role of Federal Military Forces in Domestic Disorders, 1789-1878.* Washington, Center of Military History, 1988. 372 p.

Currier, Donald J. *The Posse Comitatus Act: A Harmless Relic from the Post-Reconstruction Era or a Legal Impediment to Transformation?* Carlisle Barracks, PA, Strategic Studies Institute, Army War College, 2003. 24 p.
http://handle.dtic.mil/100.2/ADA417183

United States. Congress. Senate. Committee on Armed Services. *The Role of the Department of Defense in Homeland Security.* Hearing. 107th Congress, 1st session, October 25, 2001. Washington, GPO, 2002.

Deaile, Melvin G. *Crossing the Line: A Study of the Legal Permissibility of Using Federal Troops to Protect the Nation's Borders.* Fort Leavenworth, KS, Army Command and General Staff College, June 2003. 52 p.
http://handle.dtic.mil/100.2/ADA416373

Felicetti, Gary and Luce, John. *The Posse Comitatus Act: Liberation from the Lawyers.* Parameters 34:94-107 Autumn 2004.
http://search.epnet.com/login.aspx?direct=true&db=aph&an=14325563

Turbivile, Graham H., Jr. *U.S.-Mexican Border Security: Civil-Military Cooperation.* Military Review 79:29-39 July/August 1999.
http://search.epnet.com/direct.asp?an=2436422&db=mth

Brinkerhoff, John R. *The Posse Comitatus Act and Homeland Security.* February 2002. 6 p.
http://www.homelandsecurity.org/journal/Articles/brinkerhoffposseComitatus.htm

Center for Strategic and International Studies. *Posse Comitatus - Has the Posse Comitatus Act Outlived Its Usefulness?* by Craig T. Trebilcock.
http://www.csis.org/burke/hd/reports/trebilcock.pdf

Toomer, Jeffrey K. *A Strategic View of Homeland Security: Relooking the Posse Comitatus Act and DOD's Role in Homeland Security.* Fort Leavenworth, KS, School of Advanced Military Studies, Army Command and General Staff College, May 2002. 56 p.
http://handle.dtic.mil/100.2/ADA403866

Trump, Thomas E. *Are We Prepared to Use the Armed Forces for Homeland Security?* Carlisle Barracks, PA, U.S. Army War College, 2003. 34 p.
http://handle.dtic.mil/100.2/ADA414569

US ARMY, NATIONAL GUARD BUREAU. *The National Guard Homepage. Fact Sheets.(2005*):
Home pages. (22 October 2005)
<http://www.ngb.army.mil/downloads/fact_sheets/doc/arng_factsheet.doc>

USNORTHCOM. *Who We are: Mission, United States Northern Command Homepage (1 October 2002*): Home pages. (22 October 2005)
<http://www.NORTHCOM.mil/index.cfm?fuseaction=s.who_unified>.